ANATHEMA!
Litanies of Negation

ANATHEMA!
Litanies of Negation

BY

Benjamin DeCasseres

WITH A FOREWORD BY
Eugene O'Neill

AND AN AFTERWORD BY
Kevin I. Slaughter

Baltimore,
Underworld Amusements

ISBN 13: 978-0-9885536-2-0

This edition prepared by Kevin I. Slaughter
for Underworld Amusements.
WWW.UNDERWORLDAMUSEMENTS.COM

Bastard title page illustration by Josh Latta

A gratis audiobook recording of Anathema! *is available
by downloading it from the following* URL:
WWW.BENJAMINDECASSERES.COM/ANATHEMAAUDIOBOOK.ZIP

Further information available at:
WWW.BENJAMINDECASSERES.COM

TO

BIO

Effulgent Spirit of Affirmation

FOREWORD

By Eugene O'Neill

FOR too many years Benjamin DeCasseres has spilled his glittering fancies on a deaf American ear. He has had the fabulous adventures of a philosopher who could not abandon nor deny his poetic gift. He could not turn professional and expound a system in the thick verbiage which might awe his colleagues. Nor could he descend to the level of a daily message in juicy platitudes for the tabloid mind. In such a plight, he has had little welcome in the academy and none in the crowd. All his soaring has been lonely.

To be a true philosopher in America is almost to invite oblivion. It is only fake philosophers who thrive here. Their formula is thoroughly standardized, and only requires a persistent, brainless application. One need only have a message plain or vague enough to mean nothing and announce it with a solemn countenance and an oracular bray.

DeCasseres has always been on the loose, chasing the tail of the ultimate word. It does not matter particularly to him whether he belongs as philosopher or poet or mystic. His is a capricious mind and a vagrant one. He can be goatish or severe, ricocheting or pyrotechnical. He insists in and out of season upon recording the ascending line on the graph of his soul.

An inebriate of sonorities, he chants disillusion and raises his panegyrics to the sky. He is swift, orgiastic and inexhaustible. He cries out his negations with a huge and resonant YES! He is that phenomenal ironist who does not want to be gentle, who must be supremely contemptuous and fiercely assertive.

There is nothing native about DeCasseres in the sense that he picks up the philosophical mantle where it was dropped by his immediate predecessors. The whole Concord School and the pragmatists could have spared themselves a single furrow on the brow so far as any influence on him is concerned. Nor have any of the laborious inductive thinkers left a scar upon his mind. Hair-splitting has never been in his line. He never troubles with the question of the essential valid-

ity of ideas as such. Nor does he argue the fine points of thinking as a theory. Neither classification of causes nor explanations of them on the basis of accumulated data gleaned from the observation of the workings of so-called natural laws appear anywhere in his writings. By such definitions he is no philosopher at all.

His sources must be sought elsewhere. The scientists and metaphysicians would be quick to disown him. The mystics and poets might claim him as one of their own, but would look suspiciously upon his passion for doubt and his relentless questioning. Among them he would be a heretic too. If such genealogy counts for anything, he can be traced, among the philosophers, to Schopenhauer and Nietzsche, a hybrid product mixing despair and rhapsody.

Among the poets, he stems from the ecstatic writers of the Psalms, and infiltrates his blood with the roughhouse of the tavern. He can stand with one foot on a brass rail, raise his glass high in the air and intone a chorus, part Dionysian, part biblical, and the rest elegiac.

DeCasseres has undertaken the herculean job of carving his own niche as a writer in America. It is hardly likely that he will ever achieve wide public acceptance. Nor does it appear that he will be made the object of careful critical scrutiny by some small group *of pedants who might get a thesis out of him as an American phenomenon.*

He is too abstract for the one and too extravagant for the other. Ignored by both, his work gets only occasional publication. In truth, he is crushed between the upper and nether millstones. He is looked upon, when he is discussed at all, as a freak who is exploding with metaphors and a dazzling, colossal vocabulary. To the general reading public he is practically unknown. The schools have probably never heard his name, and would give it very scant consideration if it were forced upon them.

With whom or with what system, then, can his name be linked? What studies has he made of space and time and transcendental reasoning? To what established category can he be assigned and by what respected right has he come to the title of philosopher? None whatever. By any such reckoning, he is an outsider. He will have to get along under the designation of an unphilosophical philosopher.

When DeCasseres is mentioned in the prevailing literary chat, it is usually as the chronicler of an almost forgotten, bibulous New York. He is thought of as a post-mortem bard of the pre-Volsteadian era. In the minds of those who have only read his odes to Gambrinus, he stands for a quaint old bibber who is now reminiscing regretfully on the good old days.

Anathema! *should dispel such fantastically idiotic notions. The essence of DeCasseres' driving imagination is to be found in these Litanies of Negation. To me* Anathema! *is a unique and inspiring poem. It plagues and provokes the mind. Its vigorous figures and its exalted invective give it immense power. Racing upward, it heaps crescendo upon crescendo. It is chaotic, extravagant, brilliant, derisive with a Satanic grin and drenched with rich imagery.*

Anathema! *is far more than a hymn of renunciation. It is the torment and ecstasy of a mystic's questioning of life. The answer comes alternately as* yes *and* no. *And because the emphasis has been placed on the* no, *DeCasseres has convinced himself that he has said the final negative. It is not so. He is the "scorner of Gods and humans" and promises "salvation in a sneer." He carouses in his "inextinguishable laughter" and goes dizzy-sick on a "vintage headier than Hope." Trying to shout down the clamor in his brain with a crashing* NO, *his ecstasy overpowers him and sings its own affirmation. Benjamin DeCasseres is the poet who affirms the chaos in the soul of man. His* no *is a* yes!!

ANATHEMA!
Litanies of Negation

I WILL break every web that is woven and spin my light and my night over the universe. I will shake down high towers of thought and lay belly wise over the Ark of the Covenant in sign of contempt.

I will rend for you the arras of illusion and show you your dreams and your lives and your dogmas under the aspect of Eternity.

And seeing this, you shall wither where you stand, and labor for breath, and your eyes shall mirage the tempests of Change.

THINK you an Idea slumbers in this eternal Becoming?

Think you there is a cream-nut in the husk of evil, a core of "redemption" in the apple of life?

The "far-off divine event," long and under many guises have you of this world been taught it!

Divine and fair it is—that final event: lights out through the Cosmos, the human a-bed forever and forever!

I AM the Illicit One. My liaisons with the Innominable have spawned the imps that work in the wainscoting of your beliefs, and I breathe decay upon the rafters of your House of Certainties while you lie sleeping in your bed of illusions.

I am the Illicit One, and my cabals were held in the damp air of the Ancient Morning, before the first cock-crow of human thought.

I am the Illicit One, myself a bastard of infinite Chance who may never occur again.

I sneer at you from the zenith of my knowledge and catch you, billion upon billion of earth-flies, in the net of my thought-strands.

There I smile at you, smile at you, with a smile frost-bitten in the boreal winds of the Infinite, a smile covered with the rime of my inexorable sneer.

Ah! The humor of circles and flies!

You who are incarcerated in the finite and I who see you all in the mirror of Eternity; you who see each other as definite, palpable, familiar units, and I who see you under the aspects of Change, indefinite, impalpable, a stupendous unfamiliar repetition—do you know the terrors of this isolation, can you guess of the cold on these peaks where I have grown these bouquets of edelweiss that I bring to you down there in the mud-huts of belief?

Around the bivouacs of your beliefs and the night-fires of your sacred exaltations I pry and I skip, and from the recesses of my Beyond-World I hurl, ever and now, an arrow that rends your tents, O Philistia, and blenches your brows with the thought of me, the scorner of gods and of humans.

Could you fathom my contempt and my love for you, could you stand at the crossroads of the Expedient where I often stand, leaning on my wand of ebon—would you not then be like me? Would you not then strike tent and bivouac, no more at a Here or a There, and follow me, the gypsy of thought, the unhallowed trooper through Bad Lands and Good Lands, the implacable foe of all shelters?

But lacking humor and perspective, lacking the satanic instinct, you stick to your levels and straight lines, squat there in the morass of your beatified illusions; and it is well for you thus, you mud-moles—bait that you are on the hooks of my venomous pride!

I DRAW you forth from the scabbard of your familiar illusions, quiver and shriek as you may, and toss you into the miraculous light of the unknown and unknowable.

See you now the carnage of matter and mind they call Life? The unslaked thirst for being of the mystical Ghost of etheric climes you call God? The panorama of Change you call Progress? Ennui—the spawner of worlds? And the great flakes of pain that descend on the unimaginable generations of men like an everlasting black snow?

Then into your scabbards again, you dull, pointless ones; back to your cabals and cobwebs, you jailbirds of place, convicts of routine!

I AM the acorn of evil and the millet-seed of the Eternal. I am Aphrodite that was and the Anti-God to be. I am the cornucopia of the concrete and the glowing crucible of all abstractions. I am the Fatal Appearance. I bring you salvation in a sneer.

I am the epiphany of Oblivion—I bring you the hemlock of quiet. Drink, you who are muzzled and leashed I move in the mystery of Light. You, planet-parasites, move in the mystery of my shadow, an incalculable throng on the web your lusts weave from generation to generation.

Shall I evoke for you the spasms of pain and the sobs of long-vanished worlds, all gathered here on my heart like the dents on a shield at a siege ? Will you listen to the Symphony of the Nil? Ask rather for plague and rapine, you hedged and herded crew.

For I am the Beethoven of Negation!

I AM a monochord and I strum the eternal Nothing. I am built of the overtones of mind and matter. All intelligence finally streams toward me, and the death-rattle of the last hope shall be muffled on my bosom.

You who stand over the trough of your instincts and fatten your eyes and your lips on the slops of this world, are you not nearly sated? Will you lap up the last shreds before listening to me and acclaiming my sneer?

The Ideal and the Real—at those troughs you have fed since Time spun its webs. You are held in the vise of opposites, and gods and demons are squeezed from your vent-holes, and under a million guises you fabricate the same and the same and the same.

I have selected you, microcosms of clay, to be my butts. It is against you I hurl my inextinguishable laughter, for I am the intangible point of your every perspective, the piston-rod of your motions, the humorous imp of chagrin secreted at the core of your hopes.

From the discord of your lives I have extracted the harmonies of negation. Out of jangle I have constructed the melodies of discord.

I bring you funeral plumes plucked from the catafalques of ancient cycles of life, now rigid in nullibiety.

Let us wear them for boutonnières to celebrate the defeats of this day and the disasters of multiple morrows.

And I will assemble before you the Bacchic Chorus of Negation—Sophocles and Lucretius, Gautama and Schopenhauer, and Leopardi and Baudelaire—the Bacchic Chorus of Negation, I say, for they found an exquisite joy in their Nada! and spit from the height of their pride on the world, and grew drunk on a vintage headier than Hope.

I FLOAT before your eyes now like a vapor, a mixture of the unimaginable Ideal and the Baleful Vision.

I am an alloy. Into me has passed all the dreams of the ages. I am the apocalypse of the thing you fear.

I am compounded of you all—you my larvæ—and I wing away into the wells of light—I, taster of all honeys and nectars, quaffer of all poisons, breeder of venoms, with antenna that reach to the navel of the unborn.

With you I have labored through the Unconscious, through the waste-matter of worlds and forms, evolving the eternal Illusion—we the tools and the scaffolding, the elaborate experiment in Time of a God sick of his error, who struggles up through the morass of our souls to the citadel of our final negation.

You have sowed these myriad of æons in the furrows of the Future, and what have you gathered
but thorns and thistles that you weave into crowns?

You have woven these uncountable ages on the
looms of your hopes, and do you weave else but
your winding-sheets?

Fallow is the glebe of this world, and the shuttles
of desire are haunted by pixies of deft cunningness,
and you sow and you weave to no ends.

Out of the miraculous tomb of the past issue the
epiphanies of your countless to-morrows, which in
turn become corpses. And still, you paid pimps of
the old whore Hope, watch at that door, though
I have told you again and again that it is only the
trick-cabinet of the Master—I the implacable
watcher and challenger who loves and sneers at
you from his zenith of Knowledge.

I WAR more on the errors called truths than on the truths that you call errors. Your vices to me are more beautiful than your virtues.

Not until you are nude to the soul will I take you up into my frozen heavens.

Not until you class all truth with all error does freedom dawn in your souls.

Not until you have broken out of all tombs will I show you the irony of God.

Of me Pride has made its lordliest victim; but inasmuch as I sneer at myself and guffaw at my insight am I master of my Pride, for only Pride kills Pride.

Laugh upon laugh I launch at myself, and when you are with me in the zenith of my frozen heavens you will see me scourging myself with the whips of self-mockery.

The pride of the Nihilist! I am trapped like you all tombed in the belly of self.

I WILL muffle the gods in sleep and house myself in an acorn which shall be eternally sterile.

All gods will I turn into shadow—Apollo and the Overman to come no less.

From surface to surface, from unity to unity, I shall grow, incorporating in myself things that were and things that are.

All unities are complexities, all complexities are infinite unities. The Infinite itself—the dearest illusion of my brain, the Infinite, my spiritual itch! —shall die unto me like a shadow lost in a sea. For I am the Super-Infinite.

Where I am there shall be Nothing; where Nothing reigns there I shall be.

Circle on circle, arch on arch, span on span, cosmos on cosmos—they are nothing in my apprehension, and a single flash of a firefly is as much as the light of all suns, and the croak of a frog in a pond is the measure of all human sound that has been.

One said he had been rowed and ferried through Chaos. Another said he preached the Beyond-Man. I say I am the Chaos through which he was rowed and ferried and I am that Beyond-Man. And I say that both Chaos and Beyond-Man are the illusions of sleepwalkers.

The pride of direction in our sacrosanct seers! The vanity of origin, the vanity of end! Their tongues babble like fishwomen. I wind up their dreams on the reel of my Insight.

What mansions they build—these prophets and poets and babblers of futurity!—all at last blown to atoms in the powder-house fixed on my shoulders.

I HAVE had lewd intercourse with the Shapeless. I
have basked in the ironic glints that fell from Its
unperceived eyes.

He who is the magnet of all unities shall be the
temple of all discords.

I am the Mecca of all sorrows, the blenched and
frozen cheek on which all tears fall, the Night
unto which all secret sighs are uttered—yet am I
a Mansion of Revels, a Hall of Laughing Echoes.

I am the Mirthful Prometheus. When I have
swallowed the last shred of the Infinite, I shall
found in my Void the Dynasty of Laughter—
laughter silent, ironic, dissolving myself in its
sterile ripples.

Little brittle souls of earth—all you who come
and go, spawn of worm and ape—you will be there
with me, soul of my soul, bowels of my bowels!

THIS pastoral I pipe for you, O Philistia!—sweet XIII
fetor at my banquets, bouquet from my cesspool.
Suck I not venom from your breath like a stealthy
cat in the night? Are you not civet and musk in my
bedclothes?

"Vox populi, vox Dei!" How well I know *that*!
Shadow of the Bungler thou art, O people—the
crutch of the Blind One.

With a spring and a smirk I am among you,
winding in and out among your tents, O Philistia;
and you draw aside as from a leper, a leper with
cowl and lazarus-bell. And I pass on into the desert
and am blent with its sands and lost in its purple
shadows.

For truly am I a leper in your sight. Touch but
my garment of black and you will be infected with
thought, and through all your white tents will
stalk my Black Death: my cosmical insight, my
petrifying Super-Infinity.

I am a hangman and gravedigger. I shall wrap
you all in a shroud no bigger than the wing of a
day-fly, yet you shall be housed in the Super-Infinite, for large and small I know not.

All illusions swing like decayed corpses from the
gibbet of my Insight. I peel off the wrappings of
hope yard upon yard till the mummified Nothing starts from its nakedness. For, at last, you are
wrappings, older than time, that enswaddle me—
the uncreate Nil.

I DANCE upon the catafalques of all my dreams, become the chrysalis of fairer dreams, and emerge into my super-nothingness to become the fixed and hollow eye of Truth.

The water goes over the fall and the sun slants upon the crag, but still am I fixed in my Nothingness.

And the gods awake again, casting their filaments into the winds of the morn, and new human cycles bubble out of their mouths—but still do I keep my Nothingness.

Eden-trees blossom again, and Eves come forth from their lairs, and a myriad Christs tell their doleful tales and stagger up their Calvaries but forever keep I my rigidity.

The feudal chiefs of philosophy come unto me and find in me a sacrament of conciliation. Only those by Ganges and Brahmapootra have dreamed aright, only they have guessed me.

Epicurean and ascetic, idealist and realist, pagan and Christian are eclipsed in my penumbra, the veritable shadow of the Super-Infinite.

I trumpet beyond all suns and finger the flute of Time, swimming the rapids of all conceivable lusts, gayly dashing my brains out again and again on the reefs in the whirlpool. They are my pastimes. No hap can come to Nothingness.

I slake my thirst at many wells, and fard my face with lies, and appear as Man; or turn hypocrite, and thus become God, and tweak your brains with fair infinite vistas.

I HAVE clogged their brains with images and set them at the goal-posts of life and sped with them along their road until the little hole was reached wherein they tumbled, and I sealed them up with slabs of ice.

O Poet, hast thou seen my footprints—there on the hillock of your loftiest imagining? Have you seen spoor of me, O Philosopher, in your pro-foundest meditations? Have you guessed that the undertaker of the Infinite, God's gravedigger, passed your way?

Time and Change and Matter, those bastards of infinite shapes, are dungeoned in me, and Eternity is only one of my peepholes.

Glance through your telescopes, strain through your microscopes—all that you see, sublime and wondrous in your sight, are only fungi on my breast.

Destruction, creation—what names! I am the Great Necromancer. Destruction and creation—to me—are merely ingredients.

I reverse all axioms. Out of nothing comes some-thing, as a god is born of the air; out of something comes nothing, as all things return to me.

With the yardstick of their logic they measure the All! Buzz, little gnats of my noon; buzz out your systems here on my eyelash—sometimes I drowse and allow you to rest there and buzz.

How many times have I suspended my audience in the kingdoms of sentiency! In my anterooms and festal halls they awaited me—they the helots of Chance, the parvenus of accident. But I stayed within, interred in my thought.

They hallooed to me from without, hurling stones through my windows—sons of carpenters, fauns and nymphs, a troop from Olympus, Bacchus and Venus, Priapus and Momus, all seeking to claim me the unfettered supergod. But I was fishing from the wharves of eternity with bait cut from my brain.

And from the depths of my impenetrable retreat I heard them go away singing, the carpenter's son singing the most laughable ditty of all.

But you shall not be lost, O pale gods and riant gods and prophets with the ludicrous symbols, for with natrum and oils I will embalm you forever in my funeral parlors and you shall gossip one to the other in my catacombs in another Thebes by another Nile.

For all gods and all saviors pass over my thought like the flying butt of a cloud over the blue of the firmament.

Like that mountain near ancient Thebes where were buried kings and servitors and which bulges with its dead, so have I millions buried in me, am a necropolis of ghosts, a living mausoleum of human vanities—all housed and hearsed in me.

I walk through the woods flecked with the gold-leaf of noontime, drowsy with whispers, and the oaks bend to me, and the birds call to me (or is it I who chant gayly from their throats?).

I dandle the sea on my knee and allow it to slap me in the face with its foam as one allows a child so to do. It knows me, the space-eater, menstruum of time, avatar of the Inscrutable.

Or I leap on the back of the eagle, and when it has carried me to the confines of space I spring from its back and lave in the light of dimensionless suns.

Thus do I sport in the hippodrome of the Cosmos, drinking sometimes at the founts of the finite, lounging through the Louvres of creation, sometimes at watch from the eye of the Sphinx, or nonchalantly watching the hens warm me out of an egg. For verily I am a sportsman.

I am the rendezvous of the dead and the living. I am the trysting-place of those two lovers-in-secret, God and Lucifer. I am the clandestine meeting-place of all contrarieties.

Thoughts cling like leeches to my brain—that brain that is an eagle's nest hung on the edge of precipitous voids.

My thoughts are rungs in a ladder built in the air and which disappear in the non-existent.

When I am unapparent I am seen most; when I am abdicate 'tis then I reign. When I laugh you shall think I am weeping; when I weep you shall hear a guffaw.

XVIII   MY DREAM! What has it been? To baffle the sunlight, and stay the night, and raise the gonfalons of
negation on the time-wide debris of men's hopes,
and lead the planets, unshriven, to my abattoir of
eternities—there over the Borderland.

I have ransacked each atom seeking a Purpose,
have raked down the fires in uncountable suns,
seeking in their ashes the secret of their flames,
blended my souls with the translunar ethers, seeking to come full upon It. Only to find that I was
atom and sun and ether and the secret thereof, the
Anonymous It, the wellspring of the existent, the
final tabula rasa!

XIX   MEN have been who have said they were the
God-incarnate. Were they no more than that?

One said he was the Son of God.

I say God is my Son.

Like a ghoul, I prowl over the battlefield where
lie a-rot my dead selves, and many a gem I rip
from that rottenness, many a burnished sabre I
pluck from its scabbard.

And over the graves of my accoutred selves
grows the edelweiss.

I AM the Present, and I hold all the Past as booty.
I have pillaged the Future, and am the very core of
the coming event.

In the Infinite, Nothing changes; in the Super-Infinite, Nothing is.

THERE is no one thing better than any other thing;
there is no God greater than any other God. All are
out of the dugs of Ennui—all makeshifts, spawn
of fear and bad dreams.

Ideas are my concubines, sport of a day; then I
breathe my disgust over their faces and they wither
and pass into smoke.

To the Naught alone am I faithful—I the spouse
of the Arch-Nothing—I the port and the haven of
suns.

I have an inerasable kiss-print on my neck put
there by Aphrodite, and a glittering brand on my
forehead carved there by Lucifer, the Rightful
Heir to the Throne.

Or did I put both marks there myself? For once
I was born of the sea, and once did I sound fanfare
of revolt in the Heaven of the Philistine Boaster.

I am the mystery of memory and the puzzle of
laughter and the stretched bow of expectancy and
the rubescent stem of passion.

XXII   IN ASHY regions of the sky I bare my soul to its latter nudeness and cross the portal-gate of the unimaginable Zenith and confront the Host in his turret.

There is parley and expostulation. For this and that we lash each other, he proclaiming, I denying, each standing stark in the other's eye, there in that mystic turret at the Zenith.

I came back to sentiency strangled with laughter—my boreal laughter, laughter that is like the frozen sunlight at the poles of the moon.

What things I beheld at that Zenith, what ludicrous jargon from the tongue of that doddering old Demiurge squat in his turret!—

He the asp of the cosmos, and I the dragon that swallows the asp. He the God of the living, and I the alembic of living and dead!

XXIII   IN THE souls of men I shall leave my heel-print, ghostly, ineffaceable.

In their hearts, those claviers of pain, shall be heard forever the buzz and hum of my negations.

I am the mirthful outlaw. Through my grin you may know me, and when you hear my peals of laughter in the night rise and bolt the door, for I tread at your sill.

I laugh till I reel, and I scoff at your God, O butter-lipped, simpering Philistia!

Jezebel, Messalina, Delilah, Thaïs, Aspasia and Laïs I unleash with a laugh and bid them run wild 'mongst your tents, while I caper in motley and jig to my mirth just to see your lickerish looks and the spittle flow from your lecherous lips.

Softer than all your dreams is my Néant, and you of the earth who seek forever an Elsewhere shall find it in my breast of ice.

Humanity wears my cast-off clothes, and I mask the gods as I will.

Ormuzd and Ahriman, Apollo and Maya, Christ and Wotan—they are only visible in the spotlight of my satiric smile.

MY SOUL today is a butterfly with 'wildering wings and I have lain dormant on strange walls.

Last night I was a bat and was born of a man as he died. Tomorrow I shall be the hieroglyphic eye of a new-born child. Some days I am a gnat stinging the gods to a frenzy of destruction, and in sinister twilights I camp in the shadows and bivouac with elves.

I am the background of your dreams and the patina on your images. I am the salt in your tears and the reservation in your laughter, the mud-imbedded anchor of your doubts and the ennui that bases your happiness.

Of laughter I have strangled many times. I, too, died at Salamis, at Blenheim, at Verdun—died of the mirth that was in me when I saw the knight-errants of the Ideal fall under their banners scrawled with symbol of this and that, mouthing of God and of country.

The splendor of Northern nights lies in the winter of my eye as the aurora borealis flames over the Arctic wilderness. And if I am a Blind Pocket, then must you venture in, for there you will gather precious gems.

I will reduce you and all worlds to cinders and ashes and make of the débris pale beams to illumine my eternal night.

I am out of date, being dateless. I am old-fashioned, being primordial. I am homeless, being from Nowhere. I am a nomad, living at all points of the compass.

The Super-Infinite welcomed me as a refugee from the tyranny of Time. I was postilion in the car of the devildare gods, and was mothered on the fiery breasts of comets. All these I spurned, for in my heart was nostalgia of the Néant.

I am mankind's valet, arranging his bib in the cradle, laying out his coffin-clothes on the day of his death.

I am Life's perpetual shadow, the eternal spirit of negation and denial, sucking through an invisible hole in the rind of your hopes the juices of joy.

Not until you lose your centre are you free, not until the axis on which you turn has split will you emerge from the Wheel, not until you take from your eyes the bandage that unifies all your dreams and acts will you be ready to take my hand and enter into my Ubiquity.

You shall be Puck and Belial, the spirit of helter-skelter, a will-o'-the-wisp from the Abyss, Mumbo-Jumbo, dryad and pixy—the veritable Deus ex Machina of the Puppet-Show.

And I will crown you with my black burnoose, which will flap in the tempests of our laughter.

XXVIII   SOMETIMES stretched dreamless in my Nowhere there come to me vague murmurs from a Beyond. I lie puzzled and pallid at *that*. Can there be, then, a Super-Naught unguessed of me?

Puzzled and pallid, lying a-dream in my No-where, these mysterious whispers come to me. Am I within earshot of my Co-Eternal? Is the Petrified One taking on godhood again? Is the Great Som-nambule walking again?

XXIX   THE HOURS come dancing toward me arrayed in the purple of purpose, diademed with opals of hope, and they fade 'gainst my Doubt like sun-beams that fall into canyons.

I am a marble column veined with memories, pedestalled in the mists of Oblivion, crowned in the zenith with a gigantic Chimera.

My altars of iron are aflame with the dead—the dreaming and procreating old egos that infested my multiple selves that I plucked from their soft beds of pleasure in the heyday of their virility.

Into the braziers of Change I thrust them, and the smoke curls away in the winds, plucking at space, still seeking entity.

A funeral torch set over the cinders of my ancient abodes—such is my Thought, my last Thought, my immutable Dream.

AT THE cradle stands Hope, with seven paste stars
in her hair, her lips rouged with the blood of her
multiple victims, and over the whimpering eye of
the newborn she draws the eyelid of illusion.

The first of all midwives I call her. She stood at
the matrix of worlds and assisted at the birth of all
lies. Antidote to the worm, wardrobe-mistress of
all earth-pantomimists, high priestess who croons
her incantations from the sloughs of failure—she
reigns for her short eternity, to be finally engulfed
in my Nada.

I AM the first-born of Silence, the menacing
white-cap on the horizon of your tenderest dream.
I hang from the borders of tempests, and you have
guessed something of me at the moment of death.

Eternal Expectancy with libidinous look and
sumptuous lips, I come to expunge you and your
brats.

Like a fox, I prowl around the sheepfolds of
Philistia, carrying off the youngest to my burrow,
teaching them the slyness of me.

There they are crowned with my sinister nimbus,
taught the litanies of my Everlasting Nay, shorn of
their fleece and stood naked where the hail from
my heavens may slash at their flesh.

XXXII   HIGH over the world and its débris of thought float my black emblems from their invisible halyards.

And there beyond emblem and halyard I rise and fall in the ether, splashing my well-beloved with spray from my dreams, building my echoes in their hearts, touching lightly with my finger their foreheads, the white screen of their thoughts.

XXXIII   SHALL I break the seals on the tombs of your souls, shall I roll away the stones from the sepulchres of your griefs? Shall I draw you forth from the sack of identity and set you quivering on the threshold of my Super-Infinite?

Your souls will evaporate under my look, the close-knit pebble of identity disintegrate atom by atom in the breaking surf of my thought—surf of a sea that never spits up its dead.

I am the purple mountain which you will never reach. I am the horizon which you will never cross. I am the thought which you will never think. I am the sun whose setting you will never see.

38

THE STERILE sun of negation has reached its me- XXXIV
ridian. Strain your ear in the wind—Time itself is
asking the hour of me!

Philosophers, pedants, prophets with their curi-
ous nicknames come to the outposts of their guesses
like a caterpillar that crawls to the edge of its leaf.

Shined in pride, they walk past the forbidden
and fall into the folds of my laughter, and will be
rendered back to the earth—when I will—when
I will!

MY DREAMS are black flowers that hang from the XXXV
pale-green stems of my passion. Come you to
browse in the garden? Beware of my black blos-
soms, O mules, O cows, O swine!

Where do I hide myself? In the light! In the
light! And when will I be announced? When the
final Light falls on the starfields of Lyra.

XXXVI   I AM a hell that is tired of flame, a heaven that is
tired of joy, an Olympus stripped of its gods. I am
a pagan who spits out the grape, a Christian who
spits at the cross, and—most unbelievable of all
paradoxes!—a Jew who spits on the Golden Calf!

XXXVII   TONIGHT I am an urn wherein lie the cinders of
light. Can you read the inscription? It is a frivo-
lous one. It is in memory of the pranks of a mocker
for I have grown quite serious, become one of the
people, and orbit from belly to genitals.

Super-Infinite! My Néant! My protean esca-
pades! What balderdash, blasphemies, drivel is
this! Come, thou Philistine Venus, breedy, swarm-
ing with brats! Come, thou middle-class Aphrodite, I am in love with thy sadic chastity and thy
Christianized sighs and thy anaemic, respectable
buttocks.

And so I am redeemed, come back to the old
beaten track, sanctified in the sweat of her body, a
perfect stench of moral uprightness.

I sit with my Sorrow and exchange silences with it—that unsurfeited Sorrow that sucks at the heart of the world.

Evening came to me at noon, and its chill wind blew the flowers I had gathered out of my hand and set upon my brow a coronet of shadows.

At the time when the thrush was singing in the brake it fell upon me and felled me with its dreaded kiss.

Then in my youth, when Cupid lay in ambush behind each star, the purple arrow crashed through my heart—I the picked target of that predestined arrow from the quiver of Proserpina.

And a cowled Thing handed me the keys of a certain hell, and another Thing whose feet were shod in lead and whose forehead was a wrinkled grin gave me the password to the dungeons of grief.

And being thus parcelled among them, I went forth. And I went forth, I say, being thus chosen.

41

XXXIX   I AM evolution accomplished, the end of the road, the final negation that all affirmations mask; the heart of man's Dream; the underneath of all seeming.

I am Purpose abridged and Eternity curtailed; and from my child lips already there issued the lattermost sigh of expiring Mind.

I lie in rigid ambush behind my haphazard egos, and on the shuttle of my moods I spin my contradictory selves.

Destiny shrouds my movements in its shadows, and streamers of night unfurl from my shoulders and carry me over the borders of space.

I stand point-blank facing Eternity, forever the contemporary of Death, forever a hatcher and breeder of life.

And on the dark background of Time I engrave the destinies of races to be and efface the ancient equations and mark out the paths of the futile, ephemeral gods to come.

Sad heart of God, sad heart of Satan, I will pile up the days over your heads till the end of my whim, and then immerse you in my shadow.

The blood of the world has dried on my breast, and I am the red image of Evil, the imago of Pain, the eucharistic Pity.

I dream nebulous dreams, and they congeal and become life. I weep, and my tears drop in the furrows of the great trackless Void—seed of all griefs, poisonous kernel of all hopes.

Nothing was when I came; Nothing shall be when I leave. I am the dawnless tomorrow; the Mist wherein Memory is drowned; the outpost of Becoming; the stake and the goal of atom and God.

Life is the mask of Oblivion made fast to that invisible face with the golden threads of hope.

That mask was forged on an anvil of bronze by the old blacksmith, Necessity; and on that mask I am writ as a wrinkle that furrows the brow; or, again, you may find me in the deadly ironic line pencilled at the end of the lip.

Each one dwells in the tent of iron which he calls his ego, tent without chink, tent without slit, tent with its stake-poles driven into the depths—tent which I summon back to its ancient invisibility, splitting the ridge-pole of pride, laughing at what you thought should stand there forever—tent without chink!—tent without slit!

Let the desert keep its secret, and the Lord keep his counsel, and let them who sleep in the glacial mists of death guard their tongues. Before they were I was. On me all palimpsests are written.

Write what you may, whisper what you will— you write on the scroll of my being, you whisper into my ear.

I AM the navel of Oblivion and the eater of shadows and Time's eternal vibration. Where there is shadow I am light; where there is light I am shadow.

The Archangel of Despair, the redemptive ironic Eye of Hope, the gibbet whence swing all my apostles—can there be death for me? Is there a shroud that can cover my spaceless soul?

I stretch my ivory limbs in the marble sarcophagus of memory and resurrect as I weave my eternities. To me the future is already obsolescent, and yesterday is the bud of which I am the immortal flower.

Hope is a dawn that never gives birth to a sun— give men that as a message.

HAVE you peered into the mysterious hells of infinite Apprehension? My flesh is a porous gauze which veils magical dreams and fiery abysms.

I quaff great flagons of light from unimaged goblets. Only Death understands me, only Death and she of the twin-black lights, she through whose nature I am woven and into whose monstrance I spill my dreams, she who pinions me to her wide and wondrous lips.

I unwind her soul-filaments and bind them 'round me in great bands of love—Infinite enmeshed in Infinite, the Holy Ghost sunk deep in his chosen Virgin.

We weave, one into the other, like sun-cloud into sun-cloud, softly, passionately; there is never an end; each center begets another center, and the hours are only shadows that crumble into the days that perpetually lapse and are lost in our blasting ecstasy.

XLII My BRAIN is a marvellous silk-worm which spins universes that are tomorrowless and unbegotten in any year. There are blazoned 'gainst it strange gleams from exotic moods; I listen to the beck and call of imperious atavistic visions, the suddenly illuminated memorabilia graven on the parchment of ancient emotions.

It is in the soundless beat of thought that I embosom God, the sombre ancestor of Hell, the seducer to all decoy-heavens; and it is there that I pull away the centerpole of relativity that holds up the tent of the Absolute and am the discarnate and unsocketted Eye that sees naught but the humanly unimaginable. The muffled dithyrambs of change tenant my ear, and I have memories that were recruited in Oblivion.

My brain is a monstrous chameleon lodged in a skull.

I am a sheaf of immemorial yesterdays, the bleeding adversary of my ancestors, the cradle of a spent world.

THE YEARS have lived in my memory like a nest of tarantulas. The eternal was only the tremendous sweep of an invisible thought. My dreams, my early dreams, lied like the morning. I stand upright, rigid, in this tiny corner of the Cosmos, clamped in the black armor of melancholy.

I peopled the realm of abstract Time with an infinite number of despotic minutes, each one the tiny catafalque of a dead impulse, and lived in the marvellous enchantment of vengeful dreams.

I am an anvil, and when the mighty sledgehammer of fatality descends on me I tremble and totter——but also rise in a shower of flames into the azure.

I am without rhyme. I am without reason. I am without sense. I am without commonsense. I am. I was. I will be. I see.

THE ATOMS that make up men and mountains and heavens and suns each burst into a tiny flame and I led them at the windless hour to the very cope of Time and stood at the precipice of the Last Day. And one by one they guttered out, and I stepped into Eternity.

But I have fallen back into Time. Time—the dungeon of Titans.

Who shall add a cubit to the Infinite and a minute to Eternity? I do in the simple utterance I AM!

I have lived with kings and ancient gods and the couriers of fatality and the announcers of Life and Death and outstrip them all in my panoramic vision of Time. My flights into the light have been beyond light and I am pregnant with my selves.

My vision cannot take on matter. I am neither sculptor, nor poet, nor musician, nor architect, nor philosopher. My life is an image in a revery, and sense cannot coop what I see, nor can the atom, which is the ovary of the material, condense my infinitely fused parts.

The body, that trough of flesh wherein Time's muzzle ferrets and fishes and rends—I am not that. The frozen sun of Reason—I am not that.

The opaque center of universal light—I am not that. The godhead of Good—I am not that, nor the passionate heart of Pleasure. I am the mystery and the wonder-well of the Now, the fabulous Eye without a face, the millennium of Change.

AND THAT other God that I met on the way!

In his eyes were strangled thunders and frozen lightnings, and Prophecy was in his tongue.

He held a torch in his hand which burnt up suns.

The soul of that divine incendiary rose like a gigantic wave to a wondrous height and split against the cope of heaven and sprayed the constellations with miraculous fire.

SOME days my thoughts are like lizards that lie
motionless on the walls of my brain, stupefied by light. There are then no images that can contain my spectral intuitions, no words that can entomb my images, no ether that can transmit the light from that nebulous beyond-world.

Today, like a God, I fill the spaces of my brain with worlds, and they whirl on the ecliptic of the Infinite, brigands of space, spheres chiselled in canyons of light, globes sculpt in protoplasmic yesterdays.

I am the First Star of Heaven, and I shot my light into the passive, waiting spaces on the bridal night of the Universe.

Out of my tempest a song, out of my hell a Sphinx, out of my dreams an Eden, out of my desert a mirage of granite and gold.

AN INVISIBLE Thing enmeshes my soul, a monstrous Entity reigns in my being. I am bathed and enswathed in Silence, the silence of atoms, the silence of stars, the silence of ether, the silence of eternal, redundant generations, the silence of my invincible Self.

One thing has been since the beginning of Time: Silence. Who can be heard in the Infinite? What word will resound through Eternity? Who will fix a tongue in the throat of the Innominable?

Time hangs like a woman's hair over all essences and obscures the Unity that men seek to clasp. And dreams are dew on the leaves of rank weeds and the black plume of Death waves from each star.

Breast to breast with my Thought, I ride beyond Time and dreams and black-plumed star.

MY SOUL is a planet, and I spin rings like old Saturn. Innermost ring, thou art my body; outermost ring, thou art the Infinite. Between them lie all comprehensible measurables—deserts and cities, ant-heaps and moons, men and Himalayas.

I spin Love, Power, Liberty, Irony, the four wombs of life—and the monstrous white ring of frost-bitten dreams is one of my circumferences.

I spin death, the sleeping-room without a clock; I spin the naked glory of her eyes in the penetralia of my imagination, and I spin the ring of reticence that girdles the Almighty Symmetry.

EACH TIME my soul hatches a thought a new world XLIX is born, and from the nests of Memory I let loose the doves and ravens of my yesterdays to fly against the walls of fiery suns or to fall into the soundless reaches of my unremembered lives.

When the lightnings of my Thought illumine the sockets of my soul the clarions of the Future are muted and I stretch from nadir to zenith chiselled in fire—a glittering dagger that lies buried to the hilt in the bowels of the Dark.

I am a monstrous wave that seeks to splash the suns and toss my spray against Arcturus, and if I rise to calamitous heights it is that I may fall back and sink into the depths of the Sea and slumber on the red coral isles of her heart.

THAT ELDER year! That elder year! Where is it gone? That ancient time when I was voiceless in the Infinite, when I was eyeless in the light, and when I knew not the swollen might of the Bud that could not blossom—where is it gone?

That year, like a white star, has faded in the conflagration of my images. I stalked through Hell with the assurance of Famine, and I would have raised my rebel standard on the moon and called upon the constellations for recruits. I am the Past, yet I cannot resurrect that year that lies imbedded in Time's marvellous frostwork.

In that elder time one thought remained in my head and reared itself like a single gigantic tooth in an empty mouth, a living full-fleshed thought pedestalled on a heart of granite. And now it lies embalmed in acid—for I have done with thought.

51

I PUT my soul into the thing that passes, for only that which is transitory is everlasting. Spin and weave with the threads of desire thy impossible heavens and deceitful perspectives, O Maya! In the whirlwind of atoms and the tempest of images I am untouched, and in the frenzies of change I am the Changeless.

Only that which perpetually dies is immortal.

Precious is that which dies! Precious is that which lives for a minute! Precious is that which flies and deceives! Precious, thrice precious, art thou, Gypsy of star-lanes, mighty Itinerant, Troubadour, vagabond Spirit of spirits.

Precious am I in the sight of myself on the days I unlock the bolts of the Temple and exchange the dead lies of today for the beautiful lies of tomorrow!

Wild pulse of love, purple dreams of God, wistful faces that screen the ecstasies of memory, all things that hurry and all things that shimmer and fade are immortal in their time and matrixed in their beauty.

I am Transition—diaphanous, transfigurating, chimerical. I am perpetual in my nothingness, perpetual in my reality. I am color and light and motion, the retina of consciousness, the lying horizon of your nadir and zenith.

I MEASURE Time by the number of eternities I have
lived. Wastrel soul!

I measure Space by the number of infinities I
have recorded. Spaceless soul!

My mind is the atlas of the spiritual world. Ex-
patriate soul!

Karma may transform me, but cannot change
me. Immutable soul!

The threads of my heart trail from far-away
heavens and remote hells. O'er-laden soul!

I AM the Golden Law of Pythagoras and the cata-
leptic smile of Spinoza.

I am Progress with chimera in its eye.

I am the pendant lips of Pleasure and the epau-
lettes of Pride.

My imagination is a pharmacopæia of every sin.

My body has been strumpet and martyr and the
manger of titans and saviors.

And my dimensionless Eye of azure and porce-
lain is shot with the blood in which all life bathes.

FROM the barricade of the Perpetual Revolution I proclaim my militant Dream.

Suffer liars and sinners and trespassers and outlaws to come unto me, and in their hands I will put a flaming sword and into their brains I will inject the brains of Prometheus, Cain, Siegfried and Don Juan.

And I will teach them newer and diviner trespasses that are yet but nebulous in the consuming light of my Consciousness.

And those that are weary and heavy-laden I will teach the wild music of my seditious passions, and they shall go forth restored from the celestial purgatories of my mind.

I shall know your greatness by your transgressions, and your littleness by your compliances, and your title to divinity by the blood on your fingers.

I GIVE these thoughts of flame and ice to those who never will be born, to that impossible posterity that will never find its earthly womb, to that magical generation that will never be, to that sublime race of mortals who will ever remain faint shadows in the pool of my revery.

In the spiral nebulæ of space where colossal constellations await the seed of Time to hurtle into the ether; in the nebula of the subconscious where shadowy tomorrows laden with rich red seed of dream await their hour of exit; in the quarries of unimaged and dreamless silences, where the noiseless chisel of a ghostly Angelo is shaping out my destinies; in the microscopic universes latent in my blood—my posterity that never can be born look at me with the passionless eyes of the immortal and the dead.

Blear memories and hallucinating tomorrows come not to them, nor shall their souls turn throughout an eternity on the noiseless axles of Change, nor shall they clamber from star to star on the iron rungs of Karma, but, as antique as Oblivion, they lie stretched in the depth of a Lethe that threads its way where Time and Space are aliens.

These thoughts of flame and ice I give to them, that impossible posterity, who reign in the interregnums of Time and who perpetually usurp the throne of my soul in the royal succession of days.

Adieu to Myself, star that day cannot efface!—sun locked in its meridian!—riderless courser through incomprehensible firmaments!

Adieu to Myself, marvellous Secret folded in the gray and amber coils of an innominate Dream!

AFTERWORD

By Kevin I. Slaughter

B ENJAMIN DeCASSERES *(1873–1945), as can be discerned from the Foreword, was considered a little-more-than-obscure writer during his life. Since his death 68 years ago, there have been only a few people who have sought to revive interest in his work. Remarking on this, he once wrote "I always write as if the outside world, the public, did not exist—until someone says to me 'That's great stuff!' or 'That's lousy!' Then I know what a liar I am."*

As for the effect it had on readers, an uncredited review from The Bookman *(Oct. 1926) stated: "To read Benjamin DeCasseres is mentally to apply an electric drill. His harsh, irregular flashes of brilliance are at once invigorating, dazzling, and fatiguing."*

He did merit a decent obituary in the New York Times, *on December 7th of the year he died. It referred to him as a "columnist and editorial writer", and near the end as an "outspoken foe of communism". That they neglected him entirely as a poet is rather odd.*

He was married to Adele "Bio" Terrill on October 12th, 1919. This was the woman to whom not only this book was dedicated, but was the recipient of what was collected and published as The Love Letters Of A Living Poet *(1931).*

Of note is the fact that DeCasseres met "Bio" 1903, seeing her in passing a few times and only speaking to her once. When she subsequently moved away (with her then husband), Benjamin began writing love letters, and continued until he finally saw her again 16 years later. It was that year they married.

DeCasseres wrote for a number of different outlets, on a range of topics. His writing appeared in: The Smart Set, *edited by H.L. Mencken and George Jean Nathan before they started* The American Mercury, *where they continued to publish his writing; the magazine* Liberty; *the publications of radical Haldeman-Julius;* The New York Times *beginning before the turn of the century; and a slew of more and less mainstream newspapers and magazines.*

It was in a syndicated column appeared in the New

York Journal-American *where he reviewed the just*

released book The Fountainhead *by Ayn Rand. He referred to it as "the most original and daring book of fiction written in this country... The 'fountainhead' is the ego—your ego, my ego—which is the dynamo of all action and thought whatsoever." After receiving clippings of the article, Rand wrote to DeCasseres telling him she'd been a reader of his columns for a number of years. In fine egoist form, she added that it was "thrilling" to her to read him writing about her.*

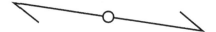

I personally discovered DeCasseres two different times, both by way of H.L. Mencken. The first time was picking up his book Mencken and Shaw *at the annual Enoch Pratt Free Library sale some years ago. I'd read the first half on Mencken, but my fascination the subject of the writing overshadowed my curiosity about the writer himself. The second time was after I purchased many bound volumes of* The American Mercury.

The American Mercury *has been an indispensable gateway to a number of unknown writers I've subsequently sought out more information on, DeCasseres included. It was an article titled "Hymn to Satan" that immediately caught my attention, and it wasn't long before I was to quote from it during a lecture on the book,* The Sorceries and Scandals of Satan *by Henry M. Tichenor.*

The quote, in part:

> *"The grandeur of America today is satanic, materialistic, irreligious, unethical... The settlement of America was the birth of a New Reality. It began the dethronement of the mystical God and the rejuvenation of the Prince of This World—prince of this world not in the Old World theological sense, but as the spirit of the Will to Material Power."*

I was so enamored by this conception of America, I recycled it for another lecture I gave a few years later in Detroit.

DeCasseres was consistent in his religious views only in the sense that he was always heretical. He rejected and often assailed atheism explicitly, even if at times his writing was rather atheistic:

> *"God, in a word, is the egotism of the atom and the egotism of myself. The atheist seeks a 'moral' God, an 'ethical' God, and not finding Him anywhere (as, indeed, there is no such God), denies the existence of God. Poor creature, you have not the courage to admire; you merely seek Justice. You cannot dissociate Power and Beauty from Good and Evil. You dare not*

affirm the beauty in Evil. Poor atheist, you are not a
brain; you are a venomous tear!"

In a critique of Mencken, he explicated his theology in the simplest terms possible: "God and Man and Nature are one and the same thing."

DeCasseres details the evolution of his religious views in another article from The American Mercury *titled "An American Wrestles with God". In the beginning he falls squarely in line with the skeptics: "Thus the child is born, and generally continues until puberty, an atheist, or, at least, an indifferentist."*

It was later in life, when puberty hit, that he paid a nickel to look through a telescope. It had a life-altering experience, to say the least. When his mind and body was literally changing, the revelation of these primordial ideas of sex and god and the universe and mankind overwhelmed and consumed him.

Only a few years later from this awakening, another singular experience focused his mind. In 1899 the South Fork Dam above Jonestown, PA broke, unleashing 4.8 billion gallons of water onto the town downstream. It was after the mass destruction and death of more than 2,000 men, women and children that he made the proclamation about God: "I consigned Him and His universe to Hell. I declared everlasting war on the Author of the universe. Lucifer,

Cain and the Devil looked like saints to me now. I did not turn atheist (I have never been an atheist). I turned Godhater. I was anti-God."

And then it was in the very next year that his brother, Walter DeCasseres, committed suicide by jumping into the Delaware River. Years later Benjamin arranged for the publication of a book of poetry written by his brother and in the introduction wrote "Walter... was a genius of the most angelic and devastating kind. Lucifer and Christ lived in the house of his soul."

Finding a writer who used such unabashed Satanic imagery (he dedicated his ongoing diary, Fantasia Impromptu, *in part, to "satanists"), and finding him by way of Mencken (a man known to have proclaimed himself a member of "the devil's party") made him instantly fascinating to me. I was quick to find that there was very little written about him, and certainly nothing as easy as a biography. Online I could discover only a few articles, or blog posts even mentioning his name.*

When he is remembered today, it is mostly for a single early poem titled Moth-Terror, *from his book of poetry* The Shadow-Eater *(1915). That one poem became a standard to be included in anthologies, notably ones manufactured for schools.*

What you now hold is a reproduction of the second book I obtained by DeCasseres. I have made a good effort to reproduce much of the typographic style of the original, though allowing for my own ability to make it better here and there and add a shadow of my own ego to it. The typeface is Granjon, and was cut by George William Jones in 1928, the same year the book was published.

And it is here, in this brief afterword, where I state my own appeal for revival. Rather than murmur these appeals to heaven or shouting them to the masses (to relieve myself of the burden), I have done as DeCasseres, and turned that appeal to myself. With the publication of ANATHEMA!, I already have multiple volumes of DeCasseres other works nearly ready for press.

Consider this the first volley of Hell-Fire.

UNDERWORLD AMUSEMENTS

The Sorceries and Scandals of Satan
by Henry M. Tichenor
foreword by R. Merciless

Men versus the Man
by H.L. Mencken
and R. R. LaMont
preface by John Derbyshire

"...a withering and ironic indictment of Christianity wrought with passion and wry humor. Slaughter's handsome re-publication resurrects an almost forgotten monument of diabolical rhetoric... The informative foreword by R. Merciless places this classic of free-thought in a historical context, listing predecessors and descendants, offering a pithy guide to literate thinkers who have embraced Satan as an image inspiring joy in life and liberty of mind."

-**Peter H. Gilmore**
High Priest, Church of Satan
Author of *The Satanic Scriptures*

"The argument of Men versus the Man is one we are still having today. The content of the argument is the relative desirability of two approaches to our social life. On the one hand is proposed a society of men: a society in which none is allowed to rise too high above another, a society that subtracts great resources from the more able in an effort to raise up the less able. On the other hand is a society of the man: a society in which individuals are left to do what they can with their inherited capabilities, in conditions of maximum personal freedom and minimal state control."

-**John Derbyshire**
from the preface

Made in the USA
Coppell, TX
11 July 2023

18980553R00042